# OUTDOOR FUN

## By the editors of
## OWL and *Chickadee* Magazines

Edited by Catherine Ripley

**Little, Brown and Company**
**Boston    Toronto    London**

First U.S. edition 1990

Library of Congress Catalog Card Number 89–63185

First published in Canada in 1989 by Greey de Pencier Books

10  9  8  7  6  5  4  3  2  1

Joy Street Books are published by Little, Brown and Company (Inc.)

Special thanks to Sylvia Funston, editor of OWL Magazine, and
Janis Nostbakken, editor of Chickadee Magazine, and to all
those people who worked with them on creating most of the ideas
and images found in this book: Lina Di Nardo, Laima Dingwall,
Jan Gray, Nancy Harvey, Michele Kraft, Elizabeth MacLeod,
Jonathan Milne, Nick Milton, Gordon Penrose, Cathy Ripley,
Wycliffe Smith and Valerie Wyatt.

Design Director: Wycliffe Smith

Designer: Julie Colantonio

Photography: Mike Assaly (page 17), Ray Boudreau (Cover,
pages 8–9, 13, 16, 18–19, 24–25, 27, 28–29), Tony Thomas (pages
6–7, 10–11, 14–15, 20–21), Peter Walker (page 5).

Illustration: Julie Colantonio (pages 7, 20, 32), Tina Holdcroft
(pages 10–11, 12–13), Vesna Krstanovich (pages 22–23), San
Murata (pages 30–31).

Printed in Hong Kong

# Contents

# Build a Scarecrow

### Here's a garden scarecrow that the birds will want to stay away from!

## You'll Need:

2 wooden stakes (one about half
    the length of the other)
Rope
Decorated head (bucket, stuffed
    pillowcase, old soccer ball . . .)
Old brightly colored scarves
Pie-plate necklace (*String several
    tinfoil pie plates together.*)
Clothes that billow in the wind
String
Nails

## Here's How:

■ Make a body frame by
attaching the smaller stake about
one third of the way down the
longer stake. Loop rope around
the place where the two stakes
meet until secure, then knot.
■ Secure the head to the top of
the long stake. (*Tie the pillowcase
on with rope, or slit the soccer ball
and push onto the stake.*)
■ Birds are scared away by
sudden motion, so dress your
scarecrow in billowy clothes.
Don't forget the scarves!

■ Birds dislike unexpected noises,
so add a pie-plate necklace to
clatter in the wind.
■ Birds avoid strings or nets that
get in the way of flying, so give
your scarecrow long string fingers
that reach down to the ground.
Tie nails to the end of each string
and anchor the fingers by pushing
the nails into the ground.
■ Your scarecrow is ready to go
to work. Try to move him every
once in a while so the birds don't
get used to him.

> ## Outdoor Challenge 1.
>
> **How can you transform a small rectangular piece of paper into a mini-helicopter?**
>
> **See page 32 for the answer.**

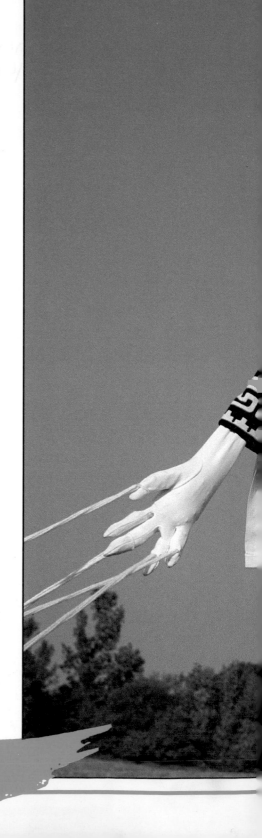

*Catch the Wind*

# Twister Kite

Make this kite out of garbage bags and sticks, and send it flying high!

## You'll Need:

2 crosspiece sticks, each 14 inches long (*Wooden dowels from your hardware store work well.*)

1 stick, 18 inches long (*This will be the spine of your kite.*)

2–3 large colored plastic garbage bags, or try decorating your own! (*Cut down each side so they all open up into long strips. Tape together end to end.*)

Scissors
Masking tape
Crayons or pen
Kite string
Bridle (*Measure out 24 inches of string and tie a loop near the middle.*)
Big safety pin
A strong breeze

## Here's How:

■ Tape each crosspiece about 4 inches from each end of the spine stick. Then tie securely with string. (1)

■ Make a string frame around the outside of the crosspieces as shown. Loop the string around the sticks many times and tape so it does not slip. (1)

■ Put the kite frame at the top of the garbage-bag strip. Trace around the frame. Add a 1-inch border around the top and sides of the tracing. Cut out along this border. (2)

■ Remove the frame, turn the strip over, and fold the plastic in half. Draw the tail as shown and cut out. (3)

■ Attach the head to the frame by taping the border edges over the string. Tape well.

■ Turn the kite over. Punch two small holes just above each crosspiece. (4)

■ Thread the bridle string through these holes. After tying a knot to secure each end, tape the holes well. (4)

READY, SET, FLY!

■ Attach the safety pin to the end of your flying line.

■ Use the safety pin to attach the flying line to the loop in the bridle, and you're all set! (4)

■ Hint: If your kite twists too much, add more tail. If you can't launch the kite, cut some of the tail off.

■ **WARNING:** *Fly your kite in an open space. Never fly it near power lines.*

## What is a Thai Snake?

**It's the largest kite ever flown. Incredibly, it's nearly as long as six football fields!**

*Catch the Wind*

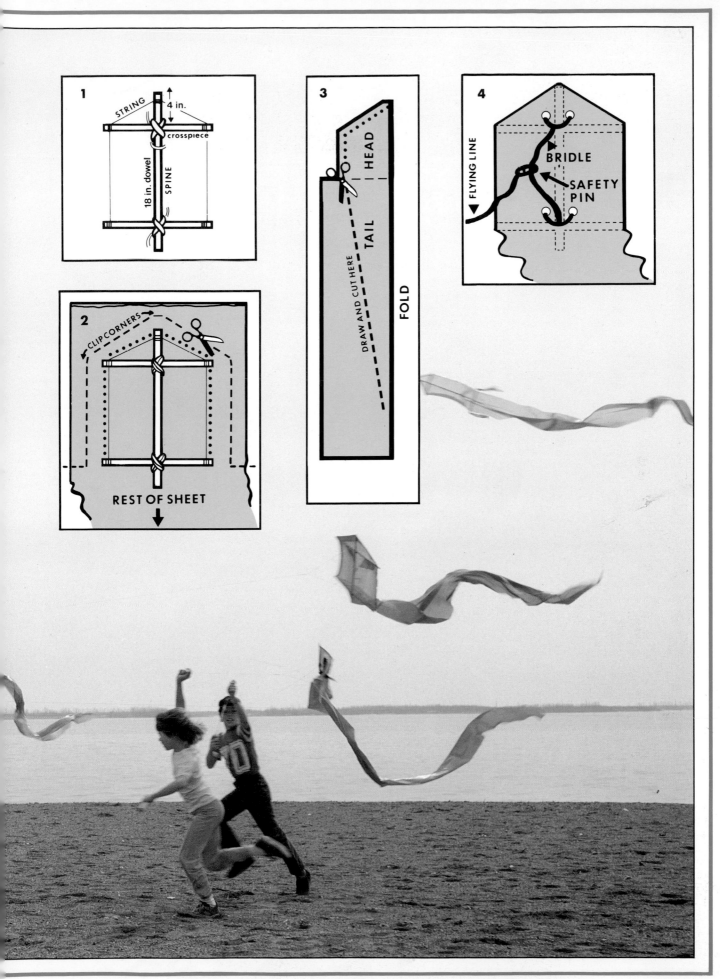

**1**

STRING

4 in.

crosspiece

18 in. dowel    SPINE

**2**

CLIP CORNERS

REST OF SHEET

**3**

HEAD

TAIL

DRAW AND CUT HERE

FOLD

**4**

FLYING LINE

BRIDLE

SAFETY PIN

7

# Windchimes

Catch the wind and let it make music for you. Hang these chimes in a tree or on a balcony – anywhere the wind blows freely.

## You'll Need:

Old keys that nobody needs (*Your local locksmith may have extra ones to give you.*)
10 feet of ribbon or yarn
Mason jar lid or coat hanger
Scissors

## Here's How:

☐ Cut 5-10 equal lengths of ribbon or yarn.
☐ Tie the keys to the ribbon or yarn pieces.
☐ Tie the top ends of the pieces to the mason jar lid or coat hanger.
☐ Hang your chimes in a breezy spot and wait for the wind!

Catch the Wind

## A Windy Day Fact

Did you ever wonder why you feel cooler when the wind is blowing? Hot food cools down more quickly when you blow on it. In the same way, the wind carries your body heat away faster than still air, making you feel colder.

# Juggling

**Juggling takes some practice, but once you get those balls rolling you'll amaze your friends and family.**

## You'll Need:

2 or 3 knotted scarves (*Start with these before trying balls or fruit.*)

2 or 3 different colored tennis balls (slit and filled with about 50 pennies) or a couple of apples or oranges

## Here's How:

■ Go outside and give yourself lots of room to practice.

■ Stand with your feet apart, your arms bent at the elbow and your palms facing up.

■ Imagine two Xs directly above your hands at eye level. When you juggle, keep your eyes on the Xs, not your hands. (1)

■ Try throwing one ball straight up, using only your lower arm and keeping your wrist stiff. Practice with each hand. (2)

■ Now toss a ball with your right hand to the X opposite your left eye. Catch the ball with your left hand. (3)

■ Pop it back the other way. Practice popping one ball back and forth until you can do it smoothly. (3)

■ Now try two balls! Hold one ball in each hand. Pop the first ball up to the opposite X spot. When the ball reaches that spot, pop the second ball to the other X spot. Practice! (4)

■ Now try three balls. Hold two balls in one hand and one in the other. Start popping the balls as with just two balls, but before you catch the second ball, pop the third. (5)

Fun and Games

**Let's have a big hand for these talented hands!**

One famous performer, Enrico Rastelli, can actually juggle an amazing 10 balls at once. Some professional entertainers also juggle knives, plates and flaming torches. Real masters can juggle blindfolded, on a trapeze or on a unicycle. Wow!

# Backyard Olympics

**These games are fun – and a challenge! Test your skills.
Which ones can you do?**

### EGG AND SPOON RACE

**And they're off! Who will keep the egg in the spoon?**

### You'll Need:

1 or more friends
Several tablespoons
Eggs or Ping-Pong balls

### Here's How:

■ Mark a starting line and a finish line on the ground.
■ For a real challenge, add some obstacles — boxes to step over, chairs to go under, trees to go around . . . .
■ Give each friend a spoon with an egg or ball in it.
■ On your mark, get set, go!
■ Whoever reaches the finish line first without dropping the egg or ball wins!

*Fun and Games*

## JUICE CAN RACE

**Who will be first across the finish line?**

### You'll Need:

1 or more friends
2 large empty juice cans for each
   friend (*Use cans that have
   been opened with a punch-
   type opener.*)

### Here's How:

■ Ask your friends to wear
sneakers so that they don't slip.
■ Mark a starting line and finish
line on the ground.
■ You all must use the cans as
stepping stones. While you're
standing on one can, you must
move the second can in front of
you and then step onto it. Move
the other can, step and so on.
■ No part of your body may
touch the ground or you must go
back to the beginning and start all
over again!

## PAPER PLATE PITCH

**Ready? Aim. Pitch . . . and try again!**

### You'll Need:

Empty box or barrel
Stack of paper plates

### Here's How:

■ Mark a line on the ground.
■ Set the box about 2 body
   lengths in front
   of the line.
   ■ How many
   paper plates
   can you toss
   into the box?

## LEMON WALK

**Don't put that lemon in
the fridge. Put it . . .
between your *knees*?**

### You'll Need:

3 or more friends (divided into
   2 teams)
2 lemons
2 large empty plastic containers

### Here's How:

■ Set up the containers 2 body
lengths in front of each team.
■ The first player on each team
puts a lemon between his or her
knees, runs to the container and
drops the lemon in.

■ The player picks up the lemon,
runs back to the start and gives it
to the next player. (This is the only
time you can touch the lemon with
your hands.)
■ If the player drops the lemon
or tips the container over, he or
she must return to the starting line
and begin again.
■ The first team to finish wins the
lemon walk.

### Outdoor Challenge 2.

**How can you make it
impossible for someone
to lift up his or her foot?**

**See page 32
for the answer.**

# Warm Up!

## These Inuit games are fun to play and great for building up your muscles.

### NAUKTAK

**"Sam's Jumping Game" is good for developing strength in your lower body.**

- ■ Lie down and put your feet flat against a wall.
- ■ Put a pencil on the floor to mark where your head is.
- ■ Now get up and crouch with your back to the wall. Can you leap as far as the pencil?

**The games you see here are hundreds of years old.**

These games were part of every Inuit child's survival training. Without strong muscles and quick reflexes for hunting, fishing and guiding dog sleds, they wouldn't survive long in one of the harshest climates in the world — the Arctic winter. Today only some Inuit kids live in the traditional way of their ancestors, but most still play these games for fun.

### TU NU MIU

**"The Backpush" develops strength in your trunk, legs and lower body.**

- ■ Find a friend and mark a line on the ground.
- ■ Sit back to back so the line is in between you.
- ■ Can you push yourself over the line first?
- ■ No cheating! You can use your hands and feet only for balance and leverage!

*On the Move*

## TILIRAGINIK QIRIQTAGTUT

**This "Jump Through Stick" exercise develops your flexibility.**

■ Hold a stick in front of you. Your hands should be about a shoulder width apart.

■ Jump over the stick without letting go and land on both feet.

■ Now try jumping backward.

■ How many times can you do it without stopping?

*Don't overdo these exercises. Build your strength up gradually. If you have back or neck problems, ask your doctor first.*

# Hiking Gear

Thinking about a city or country safari? Then take along this special equipment and be ready for adventure.

## JUICE JUG

**Make a portable cooler to keep your juice fresh and cool.**

### You'll Need:

Medium-sized milk carton
Insulation (*Styrofoam bits or shredded newspaper*)
Scissors
Chilled can or box of juice
Fastener (paper clip, clothespin . . .)
Decorating materials (optional)

### Here's How:

■ Open up the milk carton carefully and clean it out.
■ Put a thick layer of insulation in the bottom and place the can or box of juice on top.
■ Stuff the rest of the insulation around the juice.
■ Close the spout of the milk carton tightly with a fastener.
■ If you like, decorate the cooler.

## BUDDY SCOPE

**''Look at that bird!''
''Where?''
''There!''
''Where? I still can't see it.''
Now you can see what your friend sees — with a great buddy scope.**

### You'll Need:

2 empty paper towel tubes of equal size
Masking tape
Cardboard rectangle (as long as the tubes and about 1 foot wide)

### Here's How:

■ Tape the tubes onto the same side of the cardboard, parallel to each other.
■ One tube should be on the far left side, the other on the far right.
■ When you spot something interesting on your hike, look through the scope with your friend. Now you can both see it at once.

> **Imagine hiking around the world!**
> It took Steven Newman 4 years, 40 million steps, and only 4 pairs of shoes. He finished his world trek in April 1987.

On the Move

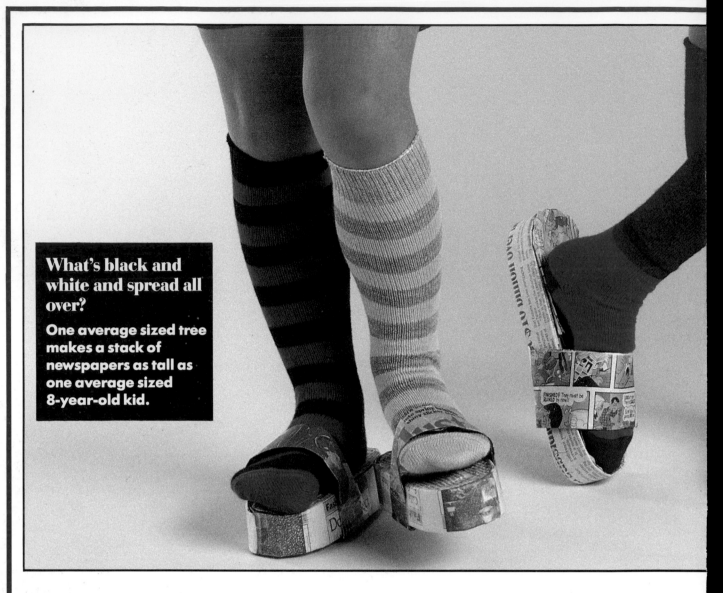

# Super Sandals

Save comic and color sections from the newspaper to make fun summer sandals for you and your friends.

## You'll Need:

About 20 newspaper sheets folded into strips about a thumb-length wide

Clear tape

White glue

Scissors

Crayon or pencil

## Here's How:

■ Wind 1 strip tightly into a narrow oval shape. (1)

■ Tape the next strip to the loose end of your oval. Wind this new strip around the oval. (1)

■ Continue winding and taping until the oval is nearly as large as your foot.

■ Strengthen the sandal by winding a strip around the width of the oval. Tape in place. (2)

*On the Move*

■ Now continue winding strips of paper tightly around the oval until it is as long as your foot. Glue and tape the end securely. (3)

■ Repeat for the second sandal.

■ Trace the finished soles. Then place each tracing over 1 sheet of colored newspaper. Cut out the traced patterns. (4)

■ Paste 1 cutout to the top of each sandal.

■ Turn the sandal over. Take the end of a long folded strip and push it in between two folds in the sole. Turn the sandal right side up and bring the other end of the strip up and over the sandal and down to the other side of the sole. Be sure to leave enough room for your foot before tucking the other end of the strip in. Secure the strips with glue and tape. Paint each sandal with thin layer of glue, top and bottom.

■ Dry well before wearing.

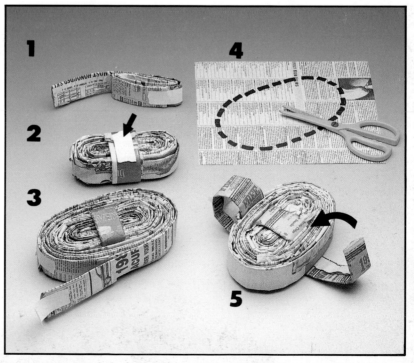

1

2

3

4

5

# On Parade

Give yourself some good luck! Make a wonderful Chinese dragon with your friends and family and go on parade.

## You'll Need:

Old, single-sized sheet (folded in half)
Scissors
Big nail or one-hole punch
Masking tape
Newspaper
Paint and brushes
Ball of yarn
Large box
White glue
Paper cups, egg cartons, tennis balls
Shiny decorations
Twist ties or pipe cleaners
4–5 hula hoops. Or take some old wire coat hangers and form them into hoops. Wrap masking tape around the place where the two ends meet. (Ask an adult to help you!)

**Outdoor Challenge** **3.**

**This book was written in the Year of the Dragon! Which animal year were you born in?**

**Turn to page 32 for the answer.**

## Here's How:

### 1. MAKE THE BODY:

■ Ask an adult to help you cut the sheet as shown in the diagram. (1)
■ Now use a nail or punch to punch holes around the sheet as shown here. Reinforce the holes with masking tape.
■ Paint the sheet and thread yarn through the holes along the bottom — the more colorful the better!

### 2. MAKE THE HEAD:

■ Cut a big hole in the bottom of the box for the mouth. Make sure you can see through it. (2)
■ Cut two smaller holes on top for the dragon's horns. (2)
■ Push rolled newspaper cones up through these holes and glue in place.
■ Paint and decorate the head with egg carton nostrils, tennis ball eyes, ribbon, tinsel or whatever else you can think of.

### 3. PUT THE HEAD AND BODY TOGETHER:

■ Overlap the front end of the sheet over the back end of the box.
■ Punch holes in the box to match those in the sheet.
■ Join the sheet and box together by looping twist ties or pipe cleaners through each set of holes. (3)
■ Attach hoops to the rest of the sheet with twist ties wherever there are two sets of holes.

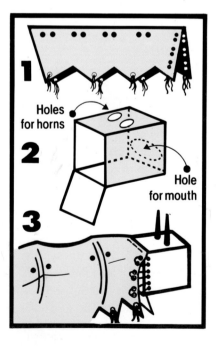

Holes for horns

Hole for mouth

*On the Move*

Satellite

Shooting Stars

ORION

3.

1.

2.

4.

# Stargazing

The next time you stay up late, look up . . . look way up and spot some of these sights in the night sky. Which one will you see first? Remember that the farther you go away from bright city lights, the more stars you'll see.

*Starry Nights*

The Milky Way

Orion

Plane

## THE MILKY WAY

This huge spiral-shaped group of 100,000 million stars is the galaxy Earth belongs to. It looks like a misty glowing band of stars stretching across the night sky.

## CAN YOU FIND ORION, THE HUNTER?

Orion is one of the constellations, or star groups, that have been mapped by astronomers. If you go stargazing between January and April, Orion is easy to see.

■ If you are north of the equator, look south for Orion. If you are south of the equator, look north for an upside-down Orion.

■ While you're looking at Orion, see if you can spot a faint fuzzy patch near his belt. This is a nebula, one of the many clouds of gas in the universe from which new stars are created.

■ Can you find Betelgeuse, an old star or "red giant," on Orion's shoulder? The redder a star is, the older and cooler it is. Also, try spotting young Rigel, a bluish-white star, on Orion's right foot.

## ORION

| 1. Orion's Belt | 3. Betelgeuse |
|-----------------|---------------|
| 2. Nebula       | 4. Rigel      |

## SHOOTING STARS

Shooting stars are not stars at all. They are meteors: small pieces of rock or dust from outer space. When one of these pieces falls through Earth's atmosphere, it burns white hot and shines briefly. Perhaps you'll spot a fireball, a really bright meteor!

### Star or Satellite?

**Any slow, steadily moving white point of light is not a star at all, but a satellite! (A plane flashes colored lights.)**

# Flying Saucers

Is it a bird? Is it a plane?
No, it's a U.F.O. — handmade by you!
The next time the moon is full,
turn some paper plates into flying saucers
and have a game of catch by moonlight.

## You'll Need:

Paper dinner plates or tinfoil pie
  plates
Plastic yogurt container (optional)
Play clay (Mix together 1 1/4 cups
  flour, 1/4 cup salt and 1/2 cup
  water in a bowl with your
  fingers.)
Tinfoil
Scissors
Tape (Clear tape looks the best.)
Bright shiny decorations and paint
  (Reflector tape, tinfoil and non-
  toxic ''glow in the dark'' paint
  and/or fluorescent paint are
  especially effective.)
Glue
Paintbrush

## Here's How:

■ Turn a plate upside down.
■ Roll out a play clay ''snake''
long enough to fit around the rim
of the plate.
■ Roll the snake on to the tinfoil
and then wrap the foil around the
snake. Set aside.
■ Paint and decorate the plate
with as much shiny stuff as you
can find.
■ When done, securely tape the
snake on to the rim of the plate.
■ Choose a night when the moon
is full and ask your parents if you
may play outside. Then find some
friends and shoot your U.F.O.
around the yard or park. Be sure
to play on a clear stretch of land
where there are no objects hidden
in the shadows to stumble over.

*Starry Nights*

■ Try out two variations on the basic design and see which one flies best. (1) Cut out a circle in the center of the plate or (2) Add a plastic container to your saucer. (Trace the small end of the container in the middle of the plate and cut out this circle. Now make tiny cuts around the edge of the hole. Push the upside-down plate halfway down the container until snug and tape firmly in place.)

**Outdoor Challenge**  **4.**

**How can you tell if the moon is getting bigger or smaller?**

**See page 32 for the answer.**

# Super-duper Dog Wash

**Follow these tips and become the best dog washer on the block.**

## You'll Need:

Warm, sunny day
Brush
Tub
Big plastic container or scoop
Shampoo (*Non-perfumed baby shampoo or dog shampoo works best.*)
Garden hose
Towels
Hair drier (optional)

## Here's How:

■ Ask a friend over. It always helps to have an extra pair of hands!

■ Take your dog and a tub of lukewarm water outside.

■ Brush your dog first to remove loose hair and dirt.

■ Ask your dog to stand in the tub of water. Praise your dog, who might be nervous, all through the bath.

■ Use the scoop to gently soak the fur with water from the tub.

■ Massage shampoo into the coat until lathery. Be careful not to get any shampoo in your dog's eyes.

■ Turn the water on low volume. Rinse your dog by holding the nozzle of the hose close to the fur.

■ Spend three times as long on the rinse as the shampoo. Any shampoo left behind can cause an itchy rash or dandruff.

■ Towel your dog down, move him or her to a dry area and let your dog sniff the hair drier.

■ Use the drier on a cool setting to blow the fur in the opposite direction.

■ **WARNING: *Do not use the drier near any water.***

■ If your dog doesn't like the drier, play with him or her while brushing the fur until dry.

### A sidewalk is like a giant nail file . . .

**To a dog, that is! It keeps a dog's nails short and trim.**

*Waterworks*

# Cool Off!

### The next time you're sweltering in the heat, put on a swimsuit and try these watery cool activities.

## GIANT BUBBLES

### Blow the biggest bubbles on the block!

### You'll Need:

3 tbsp. glycerine (from your drugstore)
1 cup dishwashing detergent
12 cups water
Large tub (*A baby's plastic swimming pool or a big laundry tub works well . . . the larger the better!*)
Sturdy giant circular blower (large plastic ring, small hula hoop, or 8 or more big plastic straws threaded with heavy string. Or ask an adult to bend a coathanger wire into a circle, then cover it with plastic straws)

## Here's How:

■ Go outside. Mix the water, glycerine and detergent in the tub.
■ Hold the sides of your blower and lay it flat in the water.
■ Lift it out slowly.
■ Hold your blower into the wind and watch your giant bubble fly.

## GLOVE SPRINKLER

### Have some wild, wet fun with a hose and an old rubber glove.

Cut off the fingertips of the glove. Attach the wrist of the glove securely to the hose with several elastic bands and some string. Turn on the water and look out!

## ICE CAPADES

### Invite your friends over for an outdoor afternoon of ice sculpting.

Freeze water or a mixture of juice and water in empty milk cartons or plastic containers two nights before. When your friends arrive, give them garbage bag aprons and challenge them to create something great out of the ice blocks . . . using only their mouths and fingers!

## A Giant Ice Cube?

**Scientists are exploring the idea of towing icebergs by ship to hot, dry parts of the world in need of fresh water. That's quite a challenge. Some icebergs are as big as the country of Belgium and tower as high as an office building!**

Waterworks

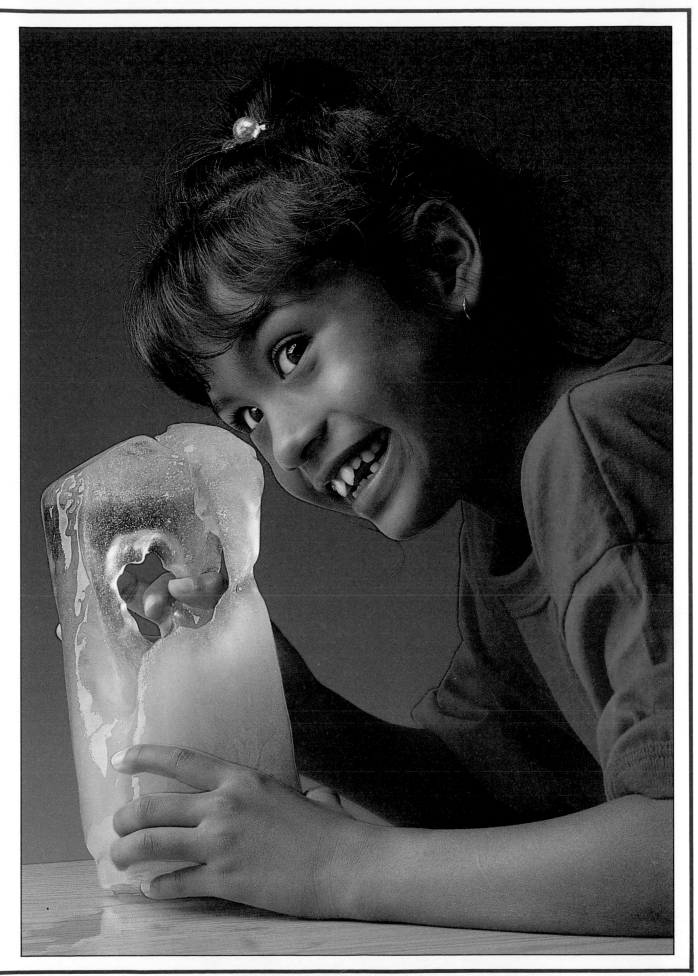

# Something's Fishy...

Can you spot why the fish in this river are in trouble? Follow the numbers on the picture and read the related clues. Which ones are trouble spots? Which things help the fish?

1. Water temperature is 55°F.

2. Kids remove garbage from stream.

3. Farmer sprays orchard with pesticide.

4. Oil spills into river.

5. Overhanging bushes attract insects.

6. Cattle are in the river.

7. A tree has fallen into the river.

8. River runs through city park.

9. Garbage dump leaks into lake.

10. There are lots of small fish to eat.

11. Sewage pipe empties into lake.

12. Pipe sucks water into power station.

Waterworks

Answers continued
on page 32.

## Outdoor Challenge 5.

**Take a look around your neighborhood. What things could you do to help the environment?**

**ANSWERS: 1.** The given temperature is just right. Fish eggs and young fish can be seriously harmed if the stream gets too hot or cold. **2.** Removing garbage makes the stream a cleaner place. **3.** Even small amounts of chemicals can be deadly to fish. **4.** Fish can't breathe well in oily water. **5.** Overhanging bushes attract bugs for fish to eat. **6.** Cattle stir up the stream bottom and pollute the water. **7.** The river swishes around the tree, taking earth and mud from under it. Deep pools are formed in which the fish can rest or hide.

31